Your Words Are
Your Weapons

Your Words Are Your Weapons

Joelle Burris

C ROSS S TAFF

PUBLISHERS, LLC

Your Words Are Your Weapons
ISBN 10: 0-9800755-2-1
ISBN 13: 978-0-9800755-2-6
Copyright © 2008 by Joelle Burris
Open Bible Fellowship
1439 East 71st Street
Tulsa, OK 74136
www.obftulsa.org

Foreword

I first became aware of the material and message that is in this book when Joelle presented it on a Sunday morning in our church in a sermon she gave. The people loved it! They got it! It worked for them! I also got it! I loved it! I think you will enjoy it too.

For months after Joelle shared this message in our church, people would come up to me and give me testimonies of how they applied what Joelle shared to their own lives. They would report that there was an obvious fresh change in their day to day circumstances when they applied the keys that Joelle shared.

For years we have had guest speakers in our church every month. Some of the finest speakers in the world have shared their best from our pulpit, but I don't ever remember having as many testimonies over such a long period of time as I have heard from Joelle's message. Now, here is that message in print. I hope the same freshness or faith and practical help will manifest in your life as it has in to so many others.

I believe this approach will bring God's order and authority to your private world in a fresh way. What Joelle shares in this book she walks out in her own day to day life and the results are obvious and reproducible.

I believe these principles are actually God's principles coming to us in a fresh package in a fresh way.

Pastor Joel Budd
Senior Pastor
Open Bible Fellowship

Joelle gives a fresh look at our authority in Christ. She has a fresh download that I believe is from heaven on how to take our authority daily and in given situations. I have repeatedly seen this work for her. She has received insight that can be understood by today's believers who are hungering and thirsting for more of God to manifest in their lives. I believe we all need to read this book and receive the in-sights that the Father has given to her. It will change all of our lives as well.

Pastor Linda Budd
Senior Pastor
Open Bible Fellowship

Other CrossStaff Titles Include:

Fill Me or Kill Me

No Longer Bound

So You Want to Date My Daughter?!!!

Use the Authority God Gave You!

God has caught my attention and taught me about all the authority we actually do have. He says this in the Bible, but my eyes have been opened to the raw truth of it. And what I'm about to say is out of my personal experience. It is very near and dear to me, and I'm really intense about it because what God showed me changed my life. I know we all say that a lot, but this time I really mean it!

What I have learned about authority has changed the way I look at things, the way I feel about things, the way I talk, and what I do. Mostly, it has changed the way I worship and pray. It's changed everything! Everything that could be changed about me internally — my thoughts and emotions and attitudes — has totally changed. It might have changed me a little on the outside, too. I think I might be walking a little differently now.

What I'm about to share with you is easy to grasp and quite elementary but very unforgettable. Maybe you already understand this whole authority thing and are using it like you should. On the other hand, maybe you never heard about it. Or maybe you have been taught about it but forgot about it. Wherever you are in this, I'm going to tell you a funny story that will make you never forget it!

I was a student at Rhema Bible Training Center as part of the evangelism group. This was the last year that Brother Kenneth E. Hagin was still teaching. I felt fortunate to be taught week after week from one of the most powerful healing evangelists. I had him for a couple of classes, and he was incredible. He embodied the message I am giving you in this book. He walked in awesome authority. He totally knew his authority in Jesus Christ.

The classroom where he taught was huge and always packed full of students. We would all be making noise and talking and laughing before class would start — and then the door would open. That instant, everyone dropped what they were doing, shut their mouths, and immediately stood to their feet in quiet respect and reverence. Nobody made us do that or even told us to do that. It was just understood because of all the great miracles and Jesus stuff he allowed to come out of his life.

We also stood because of the spiritual authority and presence of God Brother Hagin carried. If you have never heard of this man, he would be a great one to study. It is always a good thing to check out past revivals and the people God used in those events, while eagerly looking with expectancy for future fresh and new moves of God. Always have great respect for the past, especially when you get to rub shoulders with it!

Now let me paint a picture for you. At this time Brother Hagin was an older gentleman with eyes so deep they could pierce any soul. Every time he walked into the classroom, he had people walk him in and out and up and down the steps to the stage. The first thing he did was give glory to God and then he got right to teaching. He was very serious and to the point.

One day during my class with Brother Hagin, he was quoting all kinds of verses. He didn't need notes because he had taught and lived this way so long that it came from deep inside him. He would give dates and times down to the minute from fifty or sixty years ago, and he talked very fast because he had a lot to say. We were all taking notes, and he was rattling off all these scriptures and their references word for word from memory.

On this day he was speaking about the devil and how he attacks us. He was quoting Ephesians 6:16, about how our faith in God quenches all the fiery darts of the enemy. Instead, he slipped and said, "fiery farts of the enemy." He realized what he said, gave a little chuckle, corrected himself, and just kept right on going!

I looked up in shock. *Did I just hear what I think I heard?* I looked around wondering, *did anybody else hear that but me — because that is some funny stuff? Like, that needs to go on YouTube!* Some people smiled and chuckled for just a moment. I think they were afraid to laugh or were just more holy than I am, but I was losing it! I started doing that snorting stuff, where you try so hard not to laugh that you just can't stop yourself. And you know, when something is funny and you can't stop laughing, it becomes even funnier!

My shoulders were shaking. I noticed that everyone else had gotten over it really quickly, but I just could not get over it! This very spiritual, reverent man, who had done tons of crusades and healed so many people, had just said "fiery farts." I couldn't take notes the rest of the time. I think I even stopped listening and just sat there and looked at him. As soon as the bell rang I jumped out of my seat, pulled my cell phone out, and called everybody I knew. It didn't matter how funny it was to them, it was funny to me.

I won't ever forget that! "Fiery farts of the enemy!" I'm so glad the Lord brought that back to my memory when it was time to talk about authority in my church. It modernized the message a bit, which is what truth is all about! Your authority against the fiery farts of the enemy! I think Jesus had a good laugh that day, too! He has a sense of humor because he gave us one. Remember this story as you read the rest of this book. It may help you absorb the truth better.

When you know your authority in Jesus Christ, you absolutely change the spiritual atmosphere wherever you go, just like Brother

Hagin did when he entered that classroom. I'm talking about total confidence!

Total Confidence

Let me ask you, first of all, is there something in your life or anything that you do that makes you have total confidence in yourself? It might not be something you want to share with everyone...like riding in your favorite kind of car and you just feel totally cool. Maybe it's that first taste of your favorite food, and you know nobody can take it from you.

I confess it happens to me when I know I look good for the day. I have the right outfit on. Everything goes together. I put my shades on, waltz out to my car, and as I'm driving away one of my favorite songs comes on the radio. I feel like a rock star in my car! Speaking of rock stars, I have seen how people's attitudes can totally change from when they first stepped into the salon looking one way and when they left looking another way. Talk about a confidence boost—and that has happened to me, too!

I know there is a moment in your life where you just feel like a million bucks and nobody can take it from you. Right? Now I want you to think about that moment and flip it around into the spiritual realm. You need to feel that way in your spirit all the time, like, "I am a bad mamma, and nothing can come get me. Nothing can take my things!" Did you know you are allowed to feel that way?

God has given you the authority to feel that way!

I'm not talking about thinking that you're all that and being arrogant. I'm talking about being confident in who you are in Jesus Christ. This is what has been happening to me ever since I began realizing the authority God gave me.

Your Reality

Let's look at your situation. "What situation?" you ask. The one that concerns you every day. Your job. Your car. Your family. All of your relationships. Anything that is related to you that you enjoy, that you love, that you hold near and dear. That's the situation I want you to consider right now.

You know that just because you're saved and live for Jesus to the best of your ability, you're not always going to experience paradise here on earth. You have struggles from time to time. Sometimes you have struggles a lot of the time! And one of the reasons for that is because there is a devil and all his demons in this world. They do not like you, and they do things to get you off track and torment you every day — whether you know it or not. These are the "fiery farts of the enemy!"

Sometimes the enemy all-out attacks you through health issues, which is a really hard situation for most people. Or maybe your house burns down or you lose your job. Those are monumental situations to anyone, but especially when it is you!

On the other hand, most of the time the attacks can be through small things. For example, one Wednesday night after church I was really glad because I was going to get home early. I was hungry, and as I got into my car I was thinking about what I was going to eat when I got home. Then I turned the key and my car wouldn't start.

Now my car wasn't old. There was no reason it shouldn't have started, but it would not turn over. I had no warning about this. No lights had come on to give me a "check engine please" message. So now I had to call a tow truck and wait on the tow truck, which took a couple of hours. By the time the tow truck got there, it was too late to tow the car to the dealership because they were closed, and I had to take it there because it was still on warranty. So I had to have it towed to our house. By this time it was very late into the night.

My situation continued the next morning when I had my car towed from our house to the dealership. I got up early to try to have it there as soon as they opened. Then I had to wait in line for them to check the car out. Finally, the serviceman told me what was wrong with it, and I had wait for it to be fixed. When it was fixed, I had to pay for the time it took them to check it out. After all that trouble, they just had to replace the battery. This was not a monumental thing like our house burning down, but it was a total nuisance.

Maybe you had trouble with your animal this week. Your situation could have been something as small as the pet your kids love getting sick. You were leaving for work when you realized the animal had made messes all over the house, which you had to clean up. Then you realized it was so sick that you had to rush it to the vet. You had to pay for the visit, and then you had to pay for the medicine. All the while your boss is upset because you were missing work.

Whether it is your car, your pet, or your water heater, these situations are just a bunch of money-sucking, time-wasting nuisances the enemy pulls on you to steal your joy and take you away from what you should be doing. The devil's whole point in doing these things to you is to get you to swear and sin and get completely off-track with God.

First Peter 5:8 says, "Be self-controlled and alert. Your enemy the devil prowls around like a roaring lion looking for someone to devour." Simple enough, right? Let's break it down.

Be Self-Controlled

First, the Bible says to be self-controlled. Not, "Oh no, my car is broken! This hunk of junk!" And out comes everything you really don't want to say. Furthermore, you might embarrass yourself, the church, your family, and all your friends. The worst thing, though, is that you make it impossible for Jesus to do anything for you.

When you're all about you in the wrong way, having no self-control whatsoever, you forget about Jesus and have no faith. Nothing's going to work out when you're like that. You're so concerned about your situation; you don't take the time to say, "Well, these things happen. Jesus, will you come help me work this out?"

Some of us go to spiritual extremes and call the elders and the pastors and let all the saints know we've got a struggle on our hands. We call the TV evangelists and give our life savings for God to move because the devil's attacking us and this is an emergency! But that really isn't about being self-controlled either, is it?

No, you are to be self-controlled. Control yourself. This is all about the self show. And how you handle you — what you think and what you say and what you eventually do — is going to determine what happens next. Having people pray for you isn't a bad thing, but it isn't going to do any good if you don't get your own head and heart straight.

One of my favorite TV shows is *Lost*, and one of my favorite scenes deals with the power of having self-control. This particular scene is about Jack, one of the main characters, and he is a very good surgeon. When one of his friends is almost paralyzed with fear about something, he tells her what happened to him once.

During one of Jack's first major surgeries, when he was the guy in charge, he was operating on this young woman and suddenly he hit something he shouldn't have hit. Her nerves started to go crazy, and he knew if he didn't do just the right thing she could die. This scared him so badly that he stopped what he was doing and thought, *I don't even know what to do.*

Then he made a decision. He decided to let fear in for five seconds—he was going to count to five—and after that he would get back to the surgery and fix whatever was wrong. So he was scared the whole time he counted to five, and when he got to five he went back in, fixed the problem, and everything turned out fine.

What would have happened if he had had no self-control and had flipped out? That young woman probably would have died. And as it turned out, it was a simple fix. Once he calmed down and got his head back on, he easily found the problem and made things right. No law suits or anything!

I think I'm going to adopt that principle because it's not wrong to be scared. It's not wrong to have emotional reactions to bad things that happen. But it is wrong to act out of them instead of having some control over my emotions and turning to Jesus for help. So I'm just going to say, "I'm going to be scared here for a second, Jesus, and then I'm not; and then You will show me what I need to do."

When a situation happens, stop. Breathe. Take a moment to hear what the Lord has to say about it, to remind yourself who you are and the authority you have in Him. That's the place of confidence we have available to us in whatever situation we find ourselves. And when we're self-controlled, we can also be alert and aware of what is really happening around us in the natural and in the spirit.

Be Alert

Again, 1 Peter 5:8 says, "Be self-controlled and alert. Your enemy the devil prowls around like a roaring lion looking for someone to devour." To me that means, "Hello! Warning! Something could happen here. Wake up! Get prepared!"

You can't say, "Oh man, nobody told me I might be attacked. No one ever said there was a devil and demons out there, who wanted to destroy me and everything that's important to me." You can't say that because God tells you in His Word. He's telling you right now.

In my home town of Tulsa, the weather person will smile from the television and say, "It's going to rain tomorrow" or, "Tomorrow it's going to be sunny and warm." Now here in Oklahoma, as soon as you turn your head the weather changes, but the weather people do the best they can. If they say it's going to rain, then the smart people grab an umbrella or a rain jacket with a hood or something like that. They are prepared. They are alert to whatever might happen.

Unfortunately, the weather person doesn't let you know the exact moment the first rain drop is going to fall or where it will fall. They don't say, "Rain is going to fall five steps off the curb at 71st and Yale at 5:23 P.M." That would be nice, but they can't do that. So you get prepared. You wear your rain jacket or take an umbrella.

Remember Y2K, the year 2000? The media went crazy over that one. They said, "Y2K is coming. The world could be ending because all the computers are the antichrist. They are going to mess everything up. There will be no food. No water. No electricity." As a result, many people stock-piled water, food, generators, guns, and ammo. They were getting prepared, and I don't blame them.

Y2K came and went and nothing bad happened. Still, I give them credit for being prepared, and if some really bad times had come, they would have been ready while others wouldn't have.

What is the Lord telling you today? "Be alert. You have an enemy that wants to devour you." Something should be coming to your mind as you are reading this now. Life is not about surviving from one battle or hard time to the next. What are you going to do about it? It's time to get angry in the right way. Remember — fiery farts of the enemy!

He's *Your* Enemy

God is not telling you that the devil is your friends' enemy. He doesn't let you know that the devil is your neighbors' enemy or just the sinners' enemy. He is telling you that the devil is YOUR enemy. Satan wants to devour YOU.

Right now, why don't you just point to yourself, jab your finger in your chest and say, "He's my enemy." This is not complicated. You are a threat to the devil and he knows it! He's going to do everything he can to get you off track, to pollute your mind, and to get you to believe that this Jesus thing isn't working, that life was easier when you were a sinner.

Guess what? The devil is not only your enemy. He's a liar! And he's looking for someone to devour. That means he is constantly looking, searching, checking out your situation, and testing the waters to see if the conditions are favorable for him to swallow you up in fear, anger, jealousy, grief, or something else that's bad. He's watching you, waiting for you to open a door for him to come in and attack you or those you love.

I don't know about you, but I'm not okay with this — at all. Are you okay with that? If you are not okay with that, then dig deep and ask yourself, "Is there any area in my life right now that is an open door to the enemy? Is there some area where I'm not self-controlled, not alert and prepared, where I've gotten lazy or off-track?

The devil and his demons are after YOU. It is time to realize the weapons you have always had and use them. To cower and do nothing is foolishness. Now choose to keep letting the devil have his way in your life or to use the weapons of your words and turn the tables on the devil. Keep what is rightfully yours once and for all. Say out loud, "Fiery farts of the enemy!"

What's Really Important?

This is very elementary but very unforgettable. It is a vital part of the revelation that hit me. The enemy really likes to get us all stuck on the material, tangible things — the things that don't matter much in the eternal scheme of things. Think about it. We can have church in a field. We don't need comfy, cushiony chairs, some carpet, and a platform with a great band to worship God and hear the Word preached and taught. You aren't going to take any of that to heaven with you!

When I preached this message, I wore a great dress and my shoes matched my belt so nicely. It's great to look good, but it's not really what matters. I promise you, the devil didn't look at me that day and say, "Oh boy, she looks good today, so I think I'll leave her alone." I realized that what's important is what is going on in the spirit realm around me. How am I affecting what is going on in that realm? This was not dead space I was living in! What I'm trying to say is that it's not about what you can see and feel so much. It's more about what you can't see or tangibly feel.

I wish we could all have magic glasses to see into the realm of the spirit. Then we could see what is really going on in our lives, what is standing next to us, talking to us and influencing us. Is it an angel directing me or an evil spirit waiting for me to mess up and swear or give up my salvation? For me personally, sometimes I'm really depending on and listening to the Lord, and when an evil spirit tells me a lie I immediately say, "Shut up!" Other times I'm not walking so close to Him and I'll say, "What? Say it again?" It is of great importance to be slow to speak and slow to anger, leaving enough room to think purely, to discern right from wrong, and to remember what kind of authority we have.

Ephesians 6:12 says, "For our struggle is not against flesh and blood, but against the rulers, against the authorities, against the powers of this dark world and against the spiritual forces of evil in the heavenly realms." This is what matters! This is what we are really dealing with when we are hit with a difficult situation like the "fiery farts of the enemy."

Our Struggle

In Ephesians 6:12, first it says "our struggle." What is our struggle? What is *your* struggle? I know your brain automatically thinks of one area or maybe even a few areas that could use some adjusting. Be honest. If you are not having 100 percent joy, 100 percent good health, and 100 percent prosperity in every area of your life, you have a struggle going on. And the best part about that is that the Bible just told you that struggle is normal. There's nothing wrong with you! Struggles are going to happen. It is no longer a secret or a surprise.

Second, it says that our struggle *is not against flesh and blood.* I'm flesh and blood. You're flesh and blood. It's talking about people. Our struggle is not against each other, our boss, or the co-worker we cannot stand. It's not with the ex-wife or ex-husband. And it's definitely not against our rebellious kids, whom we thought we raised so well. No, it's against the demons that are influencing what these people are doing to cause situations in our lives.

Each and every one of us have struggles with other people, and most of the time we have no idea what is really going on in someone else's life. They take out their frustrations on us, and that's wrong, right? But we've got to understand that some people don't know they are being pushed and influenced and pressured by spiritual enemies who hate them and us. Have you heard the statement, "Hurt people hurt people"? They are living the only way they know how to live. So we need to pray for them, just have compassion on them, and ask God to let us see them the way that He sees them.

And third, these rulers, authorities, dark powers, and evil forces are *in the heavenly realms*. This means we can't see them or touch them. They aren't physical. They are spirits who operate in the spirit realm. The air around us isn't empty, and we determine who or what is going to have a say in our lives.

When I thought about this some more, I realized my life is not about what I'm wearing or what car I'm driving or where I live. Those things are not going to heaven with me nor will they help me get there. Those things are a blessing and are great to have, but I know plenty of people who don't require the best of the best and are much happier than a lot of people who do require all that stuff. It is about Jesus and spiritual things.

We all know this. We all say this. But do we really live this? Recently, this has become a reality to me because I've seen it work. When I have a struggle, do I get with Jesus to overcome whatever is attacking me spiritually or do I get in my own head and try to deal with the situation in the natural? Am I acting like a child of God or just a natural, out-of-control human being?

From the moment you wake up to the second your head hits the pillow at the end of the day your thoughts, words, and actions are the determining factors of where your life is headed. This now leads me to another avenue of open doors for Jesus or the devil to take control that I have seen most people don't care about. Yes, I have to go there...myspace and facebook and all other networking/socializing websites.

Just because it is free space to do with and say whatever your little emotional heart feels like, it doesn't mean you should! People please! I've heard of relationships broken because of this newer "freedom of speech," along with absurd amounts of gossip even to the max of badmouthing ministries all with the justification that says, "What? I'm just updating my page that I'm in bondage to, every ten minutes. I can say whatever I want because these are just my thoughts and opinions, and it's my right."

Now come on people, think about this. Just because you aren't saying them physically with your mouth doesn't mean they can't affect your world and what happens in it. I promise you the devil isn't as naive as this. He will use this just as much. Not only that but when you decide to post all of your junk for the entire world to review and evaluate, they have a free pass to speak whatever they want against your situation as well. So now they are backing up every negative confession you have made on yourself or about whomever you are gossiping. You will be held accountable. Let me say that again. You will be held accountable! So instead decide to use your space to uplift and encourage even when things aren't going the best. I'm not saying become one of those "faith freaks" but use some discretion. Ask yourself, "Does the entire world really need to know and come into agreement with me on this or should I war on this, just me and Jesus, and let Him perform a miracle instead of cursing myself and letting the devil have his way?" I get pretty passionate about issues like this as you can tell. I don't mean to be ugly here but I want everyone to get a spiritual wake up call. This is the time, more than ever, to wage war for yourself and to be using every weapon you have against the devil and every fiery fart he sends in your direction. You are stronger and better because of who you know your God is.

You Are God's Blood Type

Every day things either are working for you or against you. This is not necessarily your fault or your doing, but you need to realize that twenty-four-seven there is a battle going on for you between the Holy Spirit and evil spirits. The question is, what are you going to do about it? What is your part in this war?

To get to the bottom of this, you have to ask yourself, "What's been going on with me lately? What have I been focusing on? What have I been saying and doing? What have I been hearing and seeing?" In other words, what has been influencing you and what has captured your thoughts and feelings? Has the enemy got you obsessed with what's really not important, or have you been sticking close to Jesus and keeping your eyes on the things that do matter?

In order to stay focused on Jesus, you need to understand who you really are in Him. Have you ever wondered what God's blood type is? YOU ARE! We call Him Father. He calls us children. We are born of His Spirit, which means spiritually, right now, we are just like Him.

Being God's blood type is not just cool; it means there are so many wonderful things about you. Look at what the Bible tells us about this in Galatians 3:26-4:7.

"You are all sons of God through faith in Christ Jesus, for all of you who were baptized into Christ have clothed yourselves with Christ. There is neither Jew nor Greek, slave nor free, male nor female, for you are all one in Christ Jesus. If you belong to Christ, then you are Abraham's seed, and heirs according to the promise.

"What I am saying is that as long as the heir is a child, he is no different from a slave, although he owns the whole estate. He is subject to guardians and trustees until the time set by his father. So also, when we were children, we were in slavery under the basic principles of the world. But when the time had fully come, God sent his Son, born of a woman, born under law, to redeem those under law, that we might receive the full rights of sons. Because you are sons, God sent the Spirit of his Son into our hearts, the Spirit who calls out,

'Abba, Father.' So you are no longer a slave, but a son; and since you are a son, God has made you also an heir."

When I read and studied this passage of Scripture, the first thing that got to me was that we all made a choice to become a child of God in faith. We aren't robots. We didn't have to do this. God didn't force us to do it. It was our free will. We chose to be His children — even though we couldn't see Him or touch Him. It was choice in faith.

We chose to give our entire lives and to completely sell-out to a God we couldn't see. So doesn't it seem weird that we can become so devoted to this whole concept of Jesus, being a child of God, and therefore having all the rights we have — but we find ourselves having a hard time receiving healing and whatever we need from Him? We can give 100 percent to this being we've never seen or touched, but for some reason we have the hardest time asking Him for good things, accepting the fact that He wants to give us these good things, or even realizing it's okay to want these good things. Most of the time, most of us don't even ask or even think about asking.

We do the same thing when it comes to using the authority in Jesus' name that He gave us. He gave it to us because He wants us to use it! But so much of the time we don't simply because we don't know who we are as His kids, and so we have no confidence.

We need to get it into our hearts and minds that we have the same blood He has. We are like Him. We have His nature. His Spirit lives in us. We are His children, and He loves us and wants to bless us. It's just that simple. We have to know this to understand the authority He has given us and then to use it. The more we know, the more we grow, and the easier it becomes!

We Are Unique Heirs

We are all God's children, and we all have His blood type; but we are not totally alike. Each of us is unique in many ways. The verses in Galatians say that it doesn't matter what our job title is, what sex we are, or what color we are. It doesn't matter if we are a boy or a girl, black or white or red, a bank president or a farmer. No believer is better than any other believer. He calls us all one in Christ in the Spirit. But He didn't make us exactly the same in the natural. He made us all different. This is awesome! It would be so boring if we were all the same. Again, we are not robots!

God also tells us that if we are in Christ, we are heirs under a New Covenant. In the Old Covenant we were slaves under the law, doing works and making sacrifices of animals to try to be saved. But God knew we could never keep all His laws and be perfect. And I'm so glad He loved us enough to give us a better Covenant!

God loved us so much that He sent Jesus, born of a woman also under the law, to become like us, to be the ultimate sacrifice for our sins, to cut us free of the law, and to bring us under His grace. All we do is choose to accept Jesus as our Savior—believing He died on the Cross and was resurrected from the dead—and make Him the Lord of our lives. Then God forgives us, cleanses us from our sins, and makes us His child. Then we belong to Jesus and are heirs with Him under the New Covenant.

As God's children and joint-heirs with Jesus Christ, we have His blessings and authority in this life as well as the next. Since we delight in Him and He gives us the desires of our hearts (Psalm 37:4), our desires are going to line up with His Word and His Spirit. In that sense, we can have whatever we want and do whatever we want! That's a pretty good deal, don't you think?

When we are on the right track with Jesus, our desires for good things and our dreams and visions line up with His desires and dreams and visions for us. Where do you think those dreams and visions come from? The Bible says that He put them there! Our dreams are His dreams. Even the great ones that we think aren't even possible! We are all like Him, but we express what He is to us and what He puts in us differently, so we are also unique. We are unique heirs. I like that, don't you?

Superhero Authority

A client of mine told me a great story about her granddaughter. She said, "We were in the car, and she was in the front seat next to me. I asked her what she did in Sunday school, and she told me they learned about Jesus and God and stuff. So then I asked her what she learned about Jesus. She said, 'I dunno.' I said, 'Did you learn that He died on a cross to wash us from our sins so we can go to heaven with Him one day?' She paused for a minute, looked out the window, and let out a big sigh, saying, 'Well, a superhero.' Isn't that funny?"

I laughed and said, "Stop! That's not funny. That's the truth! He is THE superhero."

Let's begin to put this together. We have struggles, and that is normal. We have enemies — the devil and his demons — who want to kill us, steal from us, and destroy everything and everyone we love or hold dear. (Remember, fiery farts of the enemy!) But we are joint-heirs with Jesus Christ, children of the Most High God. Our sins are forgiven, we have the Holy Spirit living inside us, and we have God's Word to stand on. We know that what matters is what's happening in the spirit realm because that will determine what will happen in the natural realm. AND, He has given us His authority in this earth over all the evil spirits and the devil himself.

We have THE Superhero's authority!

Let me tell you just how super this authority is. I looked up the Greek words that translated "authority" in the Bible. The word used most often is *exousia*, which means "privilege, i.e. (subjectively) force, capacity, competency, freedom, or (objectively) mastery (concretely, magistrate, superhuman, potentate, token of control), delegated influence: — authority, jurisdiction, liberty, power, right, strength."[1]

My favorite is "superhuman" because it proves the Bible says Jesus is THE superhero, and the authority He has given us is superhuman. Then there is the word "potentate." I looked it up in *Webster's Dictionary*. It said, "a person having great power; ruler; monarch."[2] That's pretty intense when you think about the fact that it describes our authority in Jesus Christ.

We have "a token of control." We have "delegated influence." We have "jurisdiction, liberty, power, right, strength." The word "jurisdiction" is a legal term. We've all seen those movies where there is a criminal on the loose, everybody knows who he is, and the police are looking all over for him. Just as they are about to catch him, he steps over a state line. The cop stops dead in his tracks and says, "He's out of my jurisdiction."

When that happens in a movie, it is so frustrating! Now think about that for you! State lines and national boundaries do not apply to children of God. Jesus said He has given us His authority, He has given us legal jurisdiction wherever we go or whatever we are praying over on the earth. Now that's what I call superhero authority!

The Speech Factor

Jesus tells us He gives us authority and jurisdiction, but how do we operate in all this? In the simplest way possible: we use our words.

One of your strongest weapons to defeat the fiery farts of the enemy is your mouth. In a matter of seconds we can build up or tear down anyone or anything, and that is scary. In today's world, with cell phones, text messaging, e-mail, fax machines, and all the stuff we can see and hear on television and over the Internet, we can communicate with each other in so many ways — for good or evil.

Imagine what it would do to us if the news media started broadcasting only good, positive news. Everybody's attitude would change. Many people would be influenced to do something good for themselves, their family, their co-workers, or their neighbors. I wish that would happen, but the only time that seems to occur is around Christmas time. Unfortunately, the news doesn't report on the real meaning of Christmas, but at least we hear a lot about giving, helping people, and trying to be nice to one another.

The truth is, how often do you ask someone how they are doing and they say, "Fantastic! It's just been the best day"? This rarely happens, ever. No, they will tell you what a terrible day they've had. "You would not even believe what has happened to me!" And they pull out their long list of people and things that have made their life miserable.

People seem to love bad news, and the news media knows this. Otherwise, they wouldn't report on almost nothing but bad news. There is no better time than right now to decide to filter everything. If you are always hearing negative, turn down the volume. If you are always seeing negative, change the channel. It's time to do yourself some good and start adopting some higher standards.

Proverbs 12:18 says, "Reckless words pierce like a sword, but the tongue of the wise brings healing." What does that say to us? Our words are powerful. They change things. And maybe we should watch our mouths a little more.

I'm pretty big on words, and they are very important to me. I am a hair stylist, and where I work there are partitions with windows in them between each stylist's station. It is private and yet open. One day all the stylists were there, so there were people on both sides of me. The stylist next to me was blow-drying her client's hair, so their conversation was pretty loud. Suddenly I heard her client shout, "You're gonna get carpal tunnel!"

I thought, *Are you serious?* I wanted to leap through that window and ask her why she would say something like that. I wanted to tell the other stylist not to allow anyone to speak such words over her. Why would anyone want to be responsible for such an awful word curse?

I'm sure the client wasn't being ugly when she said it. She was a believer who wasn't thinking straight and forgot her authority as a believer, or she didn't know about her authority in the first place. And again, we have to have compassion for those who don't know, pray for them, and tell them if the Holy Spirit leads us to tell them.

In the meantime, we need to seriously think about what we speak out and declare over another person, the church, our city, our country, and the world. We may not want to hurt anyone, but in our ignorance or getting carried away in the moment we say something that releases something bad. Then some demon takes the authority of our words and does the hurt we never really meant.

Proverbs 18:21 says, "The tongue has the power of life and death." Why don't we cancel out the death part and speak life all the time? If we catch ourselves saying something negative about someone or some situation, we need to just stop, repent, and cancel out the words we just spoke. We have that authority.

One of the easiest ways we get to speaking bad things over ourselves and other people is by joking around. I was talking to somebody this week, and she was talking about her birthday. She told me how old she was going to be, and I didn't think that was very old. But then she said jokingly, "I'm gonna need a walker soon."

That was not funny to me. Why would you want that for yourself? I know she doesn't want that for herself. But sometimes we start throwing our weight around and get just a little too sassy! We need to keep a watch on our tongue and make sure we are only releasing life with the words we speak.

The Bible also says in 1 Chronicles 16:22, "Do not touch my anointed ones; do my prophets no harm." How many of us talk about our church, our pastors, the prophets, or other believers—and we are touching God's anointed with our words? Do we realize what we are doing? God warns us in His Word not to do this. We need to pray for them, forgive them if they do the wrong thing, and let God deal with them. They are in leadership for one reason or another, and no one asked us if it was okay, so it's definitely not our job to cast judgments and give our opinions as to why they shouldn't be in leadership. One benefit we do have is to learn from the good they do and from the mistakes they make. But that also means keeping a constant watch on ourselves!

In Ephesians 6:16 KJV it says, "Above all, taking the shield of faith, wherewith ye shall be able to quench all the fiery darts of the wicked." We don't want our words to become the fiery darts of the enemy that attack our brothers and sisters in Christ or our church leaders. In fact, we don't want our words to hurt anyone except the enemy.

Sometimes a Christian friend who goes to another church will call me up and tell me how incredible their services have been, and she goes on and on about it. I say, "Oh, that's awesome," but what I'm thinking is, *Just shut up!* Honestly. It's like she is telling me her church is so much better than mine. But really, who is having the problem here? I am!

My friend is excited about what is happening in her church, and if her motives are all wrong that is between her and God. He'll tell her if she is messing up. My job is to be happy with her and speak life to her, to make her day count even more. The Holy Spirit said this to me, "The common thread is she loves Jesus and you love Jesus. That is the only thing that truly matters."

What this comes down to is what we learned when we were little. We heard this in school and in Sunday school. "If you don't have something good to say, don't say anything at all." Why is this such a powerful truth? Our words carry authority, the authority of a king. So we need to be careful what we say.

Creative Authority

I have a favorite bracelet I wear quite often. Right now I'm really into jewelry that says something, and this particular bracelet says, "Life isn't about finding yourself; life is about creating yourself." Now I know there is a New Age idea out there that talks about this, but those people who are deceived are deceived because they believe they are creating themselves apart from Jesus Christ. I'm not talking about that!

In Matthew 10:39 and 16:35 Jesus said that we find our lives when we lose ourselves in Him. When we are totally surrendered to Him and He is calling all the shots in our lives, we will discover who we really are and what our true purpose is. So when I look at my bracelet and read, "Life isn't about finding yourself; life is about creating yourself," I think in terms of Jesus. I have found myself in Him; now I need to create the person He has destined me to be. How? With the authority of my words.

In Jesus, standing in His authority, my words create my future. What I speak over myself today is going to determine what I will experience today and in my future. Jesus has a vision for my life. He has dreams for me. And when I became a child of God and joint-heir with Him, His vision and His dreams became my vision and my dreams. When I speak that vision and those dreams over myself, in that sense I create myself. What He wants for me becomes what I want for me, and when I speak that out, my words make that a reality in my life.

I refuse to speak words of death anymore, over myself or anyone else. When things are wrong, I say they are wrong. I call it like it is, but I'm not going to engage in unnecessary talk or thinking that is negative and unscriptural. In 2 Corinthians 10:5 God tells us to hold every thought captive to the obedience of Jesus Christ. What does that mean? We stop the thought and cut it off if it doesn't line up with God's Word and what the Holy Spirit is saying and doing.

When we take our thoughts captive to the obedience of Jesus Christ, we will speak His will over ourselves, over other people, and over churches and cities and nations. After all, we are God's children. He created the world and everything in it with His Words, and now we create our world and ourselves with our words because we are like Him. We have His nature, His love, His wisdom, AND His authority.

What Changed My Life

Working in a salon, I'm self employed. I don't work on commission or get a salary. I rent a booth in the salon, which means I can work as much or as little as I like. However, as the Bible says, if you don't work, you don't eat (2 Thessalonians 3:10)!

I came out of beauty school and jumped right into building a business. If you have done this, you know that when you start a business it's rough. It's not about making your own hours. It's about your clients' hours. But God has always taken care of me. I've always paid my bills on time. I have always made booth rent.

Jesus has taken care of me because it has always been easy for me to be able to just sit down with Him and say, "Jesus, I trust You. You know what I have need of. Thank You for...," and I list the things I need. I know trusting and having faith is not that easy for everyone. In hard times I choose to pray like that because I feel like it reins me back in. But it is a choice. I try not to let worry and stress take me over because I know that won't do anything for me. So this surrendering thing is the only thing I have left. I know anything else I try to do or make happen will be a waste of time and energy, so why put myself through that?!

Then one day on my way to work, it just hit me that I had six to eight minutes, depending on the traffic, from where we live to the salon. My routine has always been to get into my car and immediately turn on some good praise and worship music. Maybe you already know this, but you are most vulnerable and open in your mind, your emotions, and your body in the morning. It's like you wake up and your whole being — spirit, soul, and body — opens up and yells, "Hello! Here I am! Fill me up!" The question is, what are you going to be filled up with?

Some of us get up and the first thing we do is turn on the news, boot up our computers and check what's on the Internet, turn on talk radio on our way to work or the talk shows on television if we work at home. We saturate our minds and hearts with what the world is saying, and the enemy captures us before we barely start our day.

We need to just shut that stuff off! I mean, isn't it obvious that the devil's done that on purpose? He knows the morning is a special time because the Bible talks about it. Just read the book of Psalms. David wrote, "In the morning, O Lord, you hear my voice; in the morning I lay my requests before you and wait in expectation."

Every day I would get into my car and either play some great worship music or have no music at all, depending on how I felt. I would pray as I drove to work, but then something changed. I'm not sure when it started, but one day I got in my car and just started praying in tongues. I turned on the worship music, and as I drove down the road something changed inside me. I began to pray and declare what I wanted over my day, over my life, and over everything that concerned me with a whole new sense of my authority.

Instead of describing my prayer, I'm going to give an example of what a prayer might be like and write it out for you. Then you will get a real sense of what I am talking about. It can vary from day to day, depending on what's happening in life, but you will get the idea.

I believe as you read this you will understand and feel something different.

Taking Authority Over My Day

"I praise You, Jesus, for the day. I thank You, Jesus, that the sky is so pretty, and the day is going to go the way You want it to go. You are so good, Jesus. I thank You for everything You're doing. I thank You, Lord, that today will go the way we want it to, Lord, because we are a team and we're friends and I just love you so much.

"Now I speak to my day, in Jesus' name, and I say you will be good because I tell you to be good. I speak to my clients' hair in Jesus' name, and I say you will listen to me; you will lay, cut, style, and take color how I tell you to. I speak to the product I will use in Jesus' name, and I say you will do what you are created to do, and we will have no malfunctions today.

"Today is going to be a good day. There will be no distractions or interruptions because it's me and Jesus and my clients. I pray for all of them, and Jesus, I ask You to visit them, to prepare their hearts and their souls and their minds for me, and to give them great joy and fill them with Your peace. I also pray that you would prepare my heart and spirit for them as well. Lord, give them confidence, and let them feel Your presence in every moment of their day.

"Jesus, I pray for our schedule today, that my clients will arrive ahead of time, that they will be so on track with You that they will come early and make me ahead of schedule. And I speak to my schedule now, in Jesus' name, and I say you will proceed the way Jesus and I have planned. But Jesus, I give You my schedule because You know what Dave and I have need of and You know what it's going to take to meet those needs.

"Lord, I thank You for all the clients You have sent me and for the way my business is growing. I pray You will keep away the wrong clients and take away the wrong clients if they're already here because I trust You. I thank You for sending me the right clients, the ones who will be loyal. Send me those who will build me up and whom I will build up.

"Now Jesus, today I give You my mind, my creativity, and my imagination in exchange for Yours because You are better at this job than I am. I can't do this without you! I invite You to be with me, that You will teach me things all day long in the natural and the supernatural. And this day is going to be so good because You're with me and You love me so much. I love You so much, Jesus! Thank You for being with me today."

By the time I finish praying, I'm at work. Now I'm not talking about a thirty- or sixty-minute commute here. Depending on the traffic, it only takes me ten minutes at the very most to get to work. And yes, people are pulling up next to me, wondering who I'm talking to. But with cell phones today, they don't even think about it!

The important thing I want you to know is that from the first time I did this, the minute I said, "In Jesus' name," exercising the authority I have in His name and believing every word I said, I immediately felt different inside. I became confident, joyful, and peaceful; but rough and tough at the same time.

Since then, I have discovered that no matter what kind of day I have had, the moment I get in my car and begin to pray like this, I am no longer being jerked around by my situations or my struggles or whatever else I am facing. I am also able to head things off in the spirit. What the enemy plans to make my day go wrong or create disaster cannot take place because I pray for everything to line up right. In Jesus name, I am telling my day what it will be!

Jesus Will Always Show Up

From the moment I began praying like this, Jesus showed up for me. I don't have a Fortune 500 company where I have 25 thousand employees under me. I do hair, and I am the president, founder, and only employee. But Jesus came in and overnight things began to change. It changed so fast that the other stylists in the salon noticed it before I did!

They didn't know I was praying like this every morning because in the beginning I didn't really know I was praying in a new way. I had always known that I should pray this way, but it had never really been a big revelation to me. I knew, but I didn't know. Suddenly I was feeling great and I was happy. I had more joy. I had more natural skill. And I loved to work!

Then my business flipped. My clientele changed, and now I have the best clientele anybody could ever want. I love them all. Before, I didn't like some of them. When I looked at my appointment book some days, I thought, *Urrggh, it's gonna be a goooood morning*.

Some people are not fun to be around, and some will drain you till you are a dad-gum raisin! But also, it has to do with the right fit. Jesus knows who goes together and who doesn't. And just like He sends each of us to the church that is right for us, He gave me the clients that were right—they are right for me and I am right for them. I will be honest and say I did lose some, but I also noticed I was getting good quality, fun-loving new ones just as quickly.

Whether I changed or my clients changed, one day I noticed that I loved every one of them. And I just don't have bad days anymore. I look forward to opening my appointment book and seeing what is on my schedule for the day. I smile and laugh and talk all day long. I love what I do—and I do it better and better because Jesus showed up there too!

Jesus Cares About the Natural Things

Remember, the first time I prayed that prayer I invited Jesus to teach me things all day long, both spiritual things and natural things because I work in the natural. So He began to teach me about hair. And I can tell you, Jesus does hair! He showed me all kinds of things, and now I understand it better, my skills are better, my thoughts and hands work better, and doing hair is so much more fun. He has given me new ways of doing things. There are countless times I did something to someone's hair I know I never would have thought of myself, and it saved me trouble or just made the hairstyle ten times better. It's like doing hair really started to come together and click for me.

One day some of the other stylists in the salon asked me, "Joelle, what have you been doing? We've been watching your work, and it is awesome. Some really great stuff is coming out of you."

I was totally taken off-guard. I said, "Well, I don't know." And I didn't! But then I walked away and thought, *Holy cow! It's that prayer. Jesus is answering my prayer!*

Jesus not only taught me about my job, He began to work my schedule out. When I needed to be at church at a certain time, but I had a client scheduled then; that client would actually call me, cancel, and say, "I just need to reschedule for another day." So I didn't have to call her and feel bad about moving her. It was taken care of because I had given my schedule to Jesus.

This past summer I wanted to be off work from July 3-5, which was a Thursday, Friday, and Saturday. Jesus arranged my schedule so perfectly that I did a week's worth of work in two and a half days. That's amazing! Jesus did that for me because He cares about every part of our lives, in the spirit and in the natural, and He wants to bless us everywhere.

Just Do It

Even today I have to make the decision to get with Jesus every morning and speak to whatever mountain I'm facing in my life before I start my day. In Matthew 21:21 and Mark 11:23 Jesus told us to talk to our mountain. He said that if we believed in our hearts what we said with our mouths, that mountain would move out of our lives. I don't know about you, but that's the way I want to live!

Picture your mountain. Your mountain is whatever is standing in your way, stealing your peace, or causing you trouble. Now picture yourself pointing at it and seeing it move with one word — MOVE!

If I'm going to live in that kind of lifestyle, whether I'm going to work or having fun with friends and family, I still have to make that choice to begin my day right with the Lord and talk to my mountains. And when I do this, He shows up and makes all the difference.

What are you facing today? We all encounter situations and have struggles in this life. Some of the time it's because we sin or make a mistake or go the wrong direction, and then we have to deal with the consequences of our choices. But whether we are tempted to sin or get off track in some way, the devil and his demons are behind it! We have an enemy, and we need to face it and deal with it. If we don't, we will get run over, and maybe those we love will also get run over.

Our Father God told us about all this in the Bible. We have no excuse! He has told us the truth and warned us to control ourselves, to be alert, to get prepared, and to remember that people are not our enemies. Our spiritual warfare is against "the rulers, against the authorities, against the powers of this dark world and against the spiritual forces of evil in the heavenly realms."

What this means is that we need to be spiritual when we walk in this natural world, and we need to remind ourselves that it is the eternal things that matter and not the material things. That doesn't mean God isn't interested in natural things or what we do in the natural. But when we get our lives lined up with what Jesus wants to do, when we turn everything over to Him and trust Him, and when we speak life and not death, then we can walk in His absolute, Holy Ghost, devil-busting, life-abundant authority.

When I look back and see how quickly my life changed for the better, how both my inside and my outside changed—just because I started taking a few minutes every morning to use the authority Jesus gave me—I am absolutely stunned and amazed. I mean, the confidence, the joy, and the overall prosperity have been incredible.

That is why I passionately challenge you to try this. And in case you need help to get started, here are some general points you can use:

1. Decide the time each day when you will get really serious with the Lord about how your day is going to go. It can be a matter of minutes like I have been doing or it can be an hour or two. Take the time you can and you need.

2. Play music or have it quiet—whatever works for you—and take every thought captive to the obedience of Jesus Christ. Refuse all negative, discouraging,

oppressive ideas. Instead, pray in the Spirit and meditate on God's Word.

3. Give it all to Jesus. Trust Him with everything. Lay it all down at His feet, and thank Him for handling your life, for dealing with everything you are dealing with.

4. Identify your situation or struggle. This is your mountain! You might know what it is, but maybe you don't. If you don't know what's really bothering you, ask Jesus to show you. I promise you, He wants to show you because He wants you to be free and to do absolutely fantastic in every area of your life.

5. Now speak to your mountain! In Jesus' name tell it to go and declare the desires of your heart—whatever it is you need, whatever it is you want—all those good things He wants to give you. And then praise Him and thank Him for it.

You don't have to use your authority in Jesus' name the same way I did or pray exactly the same things I prayed. Remember, we are all joint-heirs with Jesus Christ, but we are all unique. He's your Lord, and He will lead you and guide you through this process just like He's leading me and guiding me. But just do it! I promise you, you will be stunned and amazed just like I was, and your life will become something you could never even have imagined.

First Corinthians 2:9 NLT says, "No eye has seen, no ear has heard, and no mind has imagined what God has prepared for those who love him." So even if you try to imagine the future for yourself, it will still be wrong because He said, "No mind can imagine." How great is that? All you have to do is to surrender all of yourself to Him and love Him, and He will take care of the rest.

Honestly, you can't afford not to do this! Plus, what is it going to hurt? You will be in the same place you were before if you don't. Tell everything what to do because that's your God-given right. It's time to get sick and tired of being sick and tired! Time to claim what's yours, start living your life, and having fun at the same time because that's what it's about!

Testimonies

Leah Linn-

"Switching salons about a year ago, I thought to myself, how will all my clients find me? I had no contact numbers; I had to start all over. After hearing Joelle's message on talking to your day I thought, 'makes sense – let's try.' In the mornings I would come in with nothing on the books and by just saying 'I call my books full in Jesus name. Lord, you know what I need and trust you for it. Phone, you are to ring all day with clients and all the right ones.' After that, call after call just poured in. My days are full to this day and now I tell all the new girls to just talk to their days - it really does work!"

Rob Firestone-

"When you shared what you discovered about setting your day in order on your way to work in the mornings, it hit me like a ton of bricks and a light went on. See, I had been experiencing some attitudes coming out of me that I had not seen in me for a long time and it was really starting to bother me. Every little thing seemed to set me off; it did not matter what or who, from people on the road on my drive to work, people who I worked with or even customers, some of whom I did not even have contact with. I was at the end of my rope with my attitude and everything that was going on. I related to what you said that Sunday so much. As you were talking I kept saying to myself, 'yep, I feel that way, yep, been there recently,' and then I realized: Joelle is experiencing a lot of the same stuff as me.

When you finished telling us about the changes you made and the blessings you were experiencing there was no question of what I needed to do. On Monday morning I got in my truck started it up and turned the radio off. Before I left my driveway I prayed for my drive to work and all the others out on the roads going to work and school. Then I took off and started praying in tongues. Then, I prayed for the company I work at and all the people who I work with. Next I prayed for all of our customers. When I arrived at work I almost did not even remember driving there; it went by so quickly.

It did not take long for me to notice that not only was my attitude aligned right for my day but also those whom I lifted up in prayer seemed more ready for the day ahead also. After the first day I thought, 'wow this really works' - and it has only gotten better. I can tell very quickly if I did not follow this routine because as quickly as it worked to make things better, the enemy has been just as quick to try to make my day miserable.

I cannot thank you enough for your transparency and willingness to open up and share what you have learned, to help others grow and overcome obstacles in their lives. This has truly made a difference in my life and I just wanted to say thank you, thank you very much."

Crystal Patrick –

"As a single mother of two little ones, working for someone else, *and* starting my own business, I was literally overwhelmed. I felt as if waves were overtaking me, and the weight of being responsible for everything and everyone was totally unbearable. My to do-lists were not daily, but extended into the next week, even the next month! Every minute of my day could be devoted to someone or something else other than God if I let it.

When Joelle challenged us to start speaking to our morning in the name of Jesus, I accepted. She encouraged commanding my day, to let the word of God out of our mouths, to get our day in order. So I began doing just that. On the way to school in the mornings, the kids and I put on our armor of God. Then we say that this day is a day given unto God. We ask God to order our day. We pray for safety in our car. I pray that whatever I put my hands to will prosper. I wait tables. I ask that God bring into my section the right customers.

I design jewelry for my business. I ask God to bring forth creative ideas and new clientele. I pray over the pieces and ask God to release His anointing over each one. I ask God to give me the grace to accomplish His will for my life, even the little day-to-day activities. I ask Him to show me the things that are not necessary for the day.

Does this mean that every day is perfect? Of course not. I don't get everything done on my lists, but I have confidence that He has answered my prayer. What I did accomplish was what He wanted.

Another difference I have noticed is I am more God-conscious. When I commit an offense against Him, I recognize it quickly and repent. If I don't order my day, I have noticed that my heart is more hardened, and I am more prideful when it comes to acceptance of my sin and asking for forgiveness.

Joelle put something so powerful so simply. To sum up, commanding my day is an exercise in my God-given authority. I become increasingly more confident in hearing His voice. I am more aware of His presence. And my faith is strengthened because I can see more clearly when He moves on my behalf in my day-to-day living.

My life has been changed. I realize that I am a daughter of the Most High, and that comes with earthly benefits. :-)"

Footnotes/References

[1]James Strong, *Exhaustive Concordance of the Bible*, "Greek Dictionary of the New Testament," (Nashville, TN: Thomas Nelson Publishers, 1984), #1849.

[2]*Webster's New World College Dictionary*, Third Edition, Victoria Neufeldt, Editor-in-Chief (New York: Macmillan, Inc., 1996), p. 1056.

About the Author

Joelle Burris currently resides in Tulsa, Oklahoma, where she is a hair stylist at Studio II Salon alongside her husband, David. They have been married since 2007 and have expanded their family to include an emotionally expressive, twenty-pound cat named Gordon Malibu.

David and Joelle are also licensed ministers. This is Joelle's first book and she looks forward to the next adventure God assigns to her.

To contact Joelle Burris...

write:

Joelle Burris
Open Bible Fellowship
1439 East 71st Street
Tulsa, OK 74136

or call:

918-492-5511

or e-mail:

joelle@joelleburris.com

www.ingramcontent.com/pod-product-compliance
Lightning Source LLC
Chambersburg PA
CBHW071419040426
42445CB00012BA/1217